ANGLO-SAXON and VIKING BRITAIN

LIFE IN BRITAIN

Fiona Macdonald

W
FRANKLIN WATTS
LONDON·SYDNEY

© 2003 Franklin Watts

First published in 2003 by
Franklin Watts
96 Leonard Street
London
EC2A 4XD

Franklin Watts Australia
45-51 Huntley Street
Alexandria
NSW 2015

ISBN: 0 7496 4873 2

A CIP catalogue record for this book is available from the British Library

Printed in Malaysia
Planning and production by Discovery Books Limited
Editor: Helen Dwyer
Design: Keith Williams
Picture Research: Rachel Tisdale

Photographs:
Cover, title page and border AKG, Small cover image and border C M Dixon, 4
Ashmolean Museum, 5 AKG, 7 Isle of Man Tourism, 8 Bridgeman Art Library, 9 top
& 9 bottom West Stow Country Park & Anglo-Saxon Village, 10 AKG, 11 top West
Stow Country Park & Anglo-Saxon Village, 11 bottom Ted Spiegel/CORBIS, 12 C M
Dixon, 13 Historic Scotland Photo Library, 14 West Stow Country Park & Anglo-
Saxon Village, 15 top, 15 bottom & 16 York Archaeological Trust, 17 top C M
Dixon, 17 bottom AKG, 18 York Archaeological Trust, 19 top C M Dixon, 19
bottom & 20 York Archaeological Trust, 21 AKG, 22 & 23 C M Dixon, 23 bottom
AKG, 24 York Archaeological Trust, 25 top C M Dixon, 25 bottom English Heritage
Photographic Library, 26 British Library, 27 top C M Dixon, 27 bottom & 28
Discovery Picture Library/Alex Ramsay, 29 top York Archaeological Trust, 29 bottom
Adam Woolfitt/CORBIS.

Contents

Invaders!

From AD 43 to AD 407, most of Britain was part of the Roman Empire. Only Scotland stayed free from Roman control. But after around AD 370, Roman lands throughout Europe were invaded by warriors from Central Asia. They defeated the Romans in battle, and attacked the great city of Rome. Roman armies left Britain, to defend their capital city.

The last Roman soldiers sailed away from Britain in AD 407. Now the Britons – the people of Britain – were ruled by local kings. The kings who lived where the Romans once ruled spoke Latin (the Roman language) and lived in Roman style. Each had his own private army. The British warriors were brave, but were not as well trained or equipped as Roman troops had been.

The Saxons search for land

Once the Romans had gone, Britain was in danger. For several years, warships sailed by Saxons – a people from Germany – had raided its southern coast, looking for anything valuable to carry away.

By around AD 600, thousands of Saxon families had arrived to settle in Britain, along with other peoples from northern Europe – Angles and Jutes from Denmark, and Frisians from Holland.

◀ The 'Alfred Jewel' – a gold and enamel pointer used to follow lines of text in books. It is decorated with a portrait of Saxon King Alfred the Great, and the words 'Alfred had me made'. Alfred, who ruled from AD 871 to 899, is the first known king of England who could read and write. The pointer was found in Somerset and is now in the Ashmolean Museum in Oxford.

These peoples eventually controlled most of England. Today we call them 'Anglo-Saxons' or simply, 'Saxons'.

Viking raiders and settlers

Just 200 years later, new invaders threatened Britain. These were Vikings, bold raiders who sailed from Norway and Denmark to attack peaceful towns and villages in many parts of Europe. They made their first raid on Britain in AD 789, and their last in AD 1085. Viking families also settled in northern and eastern England, northern Scotland, Orkney, Shetland, the Hebrides and south-east Ireland.

Closely related peoples

Saxon and Viking people came from neighbouring regions of northern Europe. They spoke closely related languages, and shared similar values and beliefs. Their lifestyles were the same in many ways. However, there were differences between them and you can find out about some of these as you read through this book.

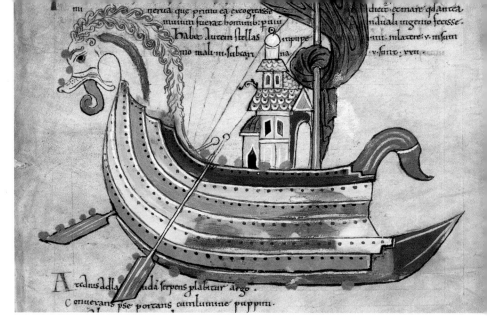

▲ A Viking warship as painted in an 11th-century Saxon manuscript, now in the British Library. Viking raiders sailed from Scandinavia to Britain in fast, seaworthy ships, crewed by powerful warriors. They wanted treasure, captives and new land to farm.

▼ Saxon and Viking invaders first settled in the east, then gradually moved to live in many other regions of the British Isles.

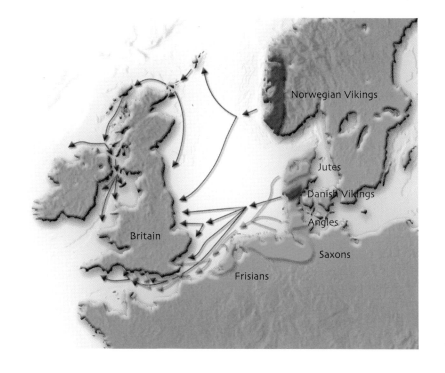

Norwegian Vikings

Jutes

Danish Vikings

Angles

Britain

Saxons

Frisians

Kings and People

The Saxons and Vikings lived in violent times. Their leaders fought for the right to rule. They won followers by giving them land, slaves and treasure. If a lord became old and weak, his followers might leave him, and seek protection from another, stronger, lord.

By around AD 700, Saxon warlords controlled the whole of England. The strongest rulers called themselves kings. The first Saxon kings ruled only small areas of land, and spent their time fighting the Britons, who tried to drive them away. By around AD 800, Saxons had set up seven strong kingdoms in England.

Establishing the Danelaw

The first Viking raids on Britain were also led by individual chiefs, but after about AD 865 Viking invaders were organized into one large army, commanded by a single king. The Saxons who fought against them were led by Alfred the Great, king of Wessex.

▶ This map shows the seven kingdoms of Saxon England around AD 800, just before the main Viking invasions began. These kingdoms were often at war. During the reign of King Offa (ruled AD 757 –796) Mercia became the strongest kingdom, and controlled East Anglia, Essex, Sussex and Kent. After Alfred successfully halted the Viking attack in AD 878, his kingdom of Wessex was the most powerful.

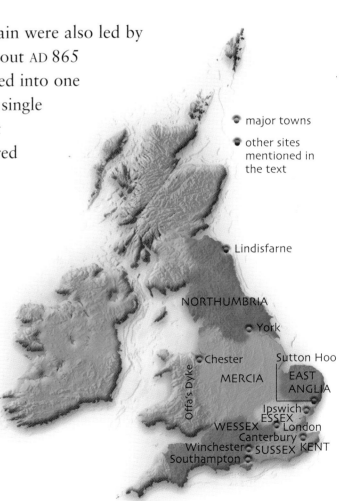

- major towns
- other sites mentioned in the text

Lindisfarne

NORTHUMBRIA

York

Chester

Sutton Hoo

Offa's Dyke

MERCIA

EAST ANGLIA

Ipswich

ESSEX

WESSEX

London

Canterbury

Winchester

SUSSEX KENT

Southampton

▶ On this map the areas of Viking settlement in Britain are shown in yellow. From around AD 865 until 1042, north-east England became a Viking kingdom, known as the Danelaw. Parts of northern Scotland and the nearby islands remained under Viking control for a further 400 years. Today, almost half the people in Shetland are partly descended from Vikings who came from Norway.

SHETLAND
Jarlshof

ORKNEY

ISLE OF LEWIS
Arnol

● major towns
● other sites mentioned in the text

Whithorn

Ribblehead

ISLE OF MAN
York

Dublin

D A N E L A W
Lincoln
Derby   Nottingham
Leicester   Norwich
Thetford
Stamford   Ipswich

In AD 878 Alfred agreed a peace treaty with the Viking king, Guthrum. For the next 200 years, the Vikings ruled north-eastern England, which became known as the 'Danelaw'. Saxon kings ruled the south and west while British kings continued to rule most of Scotland, Wales and Ireland.

DIVIDED SOCIETIES

Saxon and Viking society was divided into three main groups – nobles, free people and slaves. Nobles and free people owed loyalty to the lord who protected them, and to their local community. Slaves belonged to their owners, and were not free to leave.

◀ The Tynwald (parliament), which began in Viking times, is still held held every year on the Isle of Man. Wherever they settled, Viking people took their own laws and customs with them. These included local parliaments, where people could meet to settle quarrels, punish criminals and make new laws. But they were also occasions for meeting old friends, strolling around merchants' stalls, drinking and having fun.

Family Life

All the members of Saxon and Viking families were kept very busy. Both young and old had their own jobs to do and tasks to carry out. They were also expected to help each other when the need arose.

Saxon and Viking children were expected to make themselves useful. They helped their parents and learned practical skills, such as cooking and weaving (for girls) or fighting and fishing (for boys). There were no schools. Between 12 and 15 years old, girls got married, and boys joined a warlord's army, or started to work full-time on the farm.

WOMEN'S RIGHTS

Men were more powerful than women in Saxon and Viking times, but women did have some legal rights. They could not be married against their will, could own land and goods, and, in pre-Christian times, could seek a divorce. Many women were left in charge of farms while their husbands were away fighting. But women could not sail on warships, and some jobs such as iron-worker, poet or stone-carver were closed to them.

◄ Emma, or Aelfgifu (on the left of the altar), was the powerful wife of King Cnut (opposite her on the right). He ruled a large empire in Britain and Scandinavia. After Cnut died in 1035, their son, Harthacnut, became king of England in 1040. Emma helped him rule. This illustration comes from a religious manuscript now in the British Library.

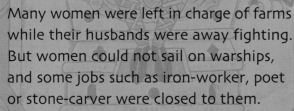

Caring for the weak

When people grew too old to work, or fell ill or got injured, it was the duty of family members to look after them. Some Saxon and Viking families could be very hard-hearted, though. Weak or sickly babies might be left out in the cold to die and if food ran short in winter, old people might not be fed.

Family feuds

Family honour was very important. If a family member was killed, relatives demanded money or goods in compensation from the killer. If the killer refused to pay, the victim's family attacked him – and his innocent relatives. They, in turn, fought back, killing as many of the attacker's family as they could find. **Feuds** like this could continue for generations, especially among the Vikings.

▲ ▶ At West Stow in Suffolk people today recreate the daily life of the Saxons for visitors.

Saxon and Viking women made most of the clothes worn by their families. They spun strands of wool or flax into thread, wove them into cloth, then stitched lengths of cloth together.

Saxon and Viking men used local materials – such as timber (for furniture) and tough plant fibres (for nets and ropes) – to make tools and equipment.

Farming, Hunting, Fishing, Food

Most Saxon and Viking families lived in the countryside, and worked on the land. They had to provide food for themselves, with some left over to sell or to give to their lords as taxes.

Farmers reared sheep for meat, milk and wool, and goats and pigs for meat. Ducks, geese and chickens provided them with eggs. Farmers also grew apples and pears in orchards, and a few vegetables such as peas, onions and cabbages. Grain, to make bread, was their most important crop. Wheat grew best in southern Britain, while oats and barley were more suited to the north.

Sharing the land

In early Saxon times, and in places where the Vikings settled, each family owned its own plot of land to grow food. This was often in big fields, where each family had a share of good and bad soil. The families shared hay meadows and rough pasture land.

▲ A manuscript illustration of farmers at work in January, drawn around 1050 and now in the British Library. Farmers used a wooden plough, tipped with a sharp blade of iron, to break up the surface of their fields, ready for planting seeds of oats, barley, wheat or rye. A team of oxen pulled the plough.

In later Saxon times, powerful lords claimed the right to own all the land. They made ordinary people work for them on their big estates, in return for the right to live on their own small plots.

Saxon and Viking women concocted medicines from mixtures of herbs, fried in butter or stewed. Many were horribly bitter, but 'garlic in hen broth' sounds quite tasty, and was said to be good for digestive troubles. So was this recipe: 'For heaviness in the belly, give to eat radish with salt, and sips of vinegar. Soon his mood will lighten.'

▼ At the reconstructed Saxon village of West Stow in Suffolk, a man dressed in Saxon costume makes a bow. Saxons and Vikings shot deer and wild boar with bows and arrows. They also fished in rivers and around the coast and set traps for hares and wild birds. Wild berries, leaves, nuts, mushrooms, seaweed and honey were gathered and eaten, too.

Making food and drink

Women cooked food and baked bread over open fires. They made butter and cheese in wooden churns, and preserved food for the winter by steeping it in salt water, drying it in the sun, or hanging it in wood-smoke. Favourite drinks were **mead** and ale, both made by leaving the ingredients to **ferment**. Mead was made from honey and ale from grains.

▶ Farmhouses, such as this one at Arnol on the Isle of Lewis, were built with plenty of storage space close by, so that food could be safely kept to eat in the cold winter months. There were no refrigerators in Saxon and Viking times, but the Vikings may have used deep snow as a natural refrigerator.

Houses and Great Halls

Both Saxon and Viking houses in Britain were just one storey high, with two or three rooms divided by wooden partitions. They were very dark inside, because they had no windows – only a heavy wooden door, which was barred shut at night and in winter time.

Early Saxon houses were square or oblong, and built over sunken pits covered by wooden plank floors. The pits were probably used for storage. Later Saxon houses were built without pits, and their floors were made of pounded clay, cobbles (rounded stones), or well-trodden earth. Viking homes were often longhouses – very long, narrow buildings, with rooms for the family at one end and byres (stables) for horses and cattle at the other.

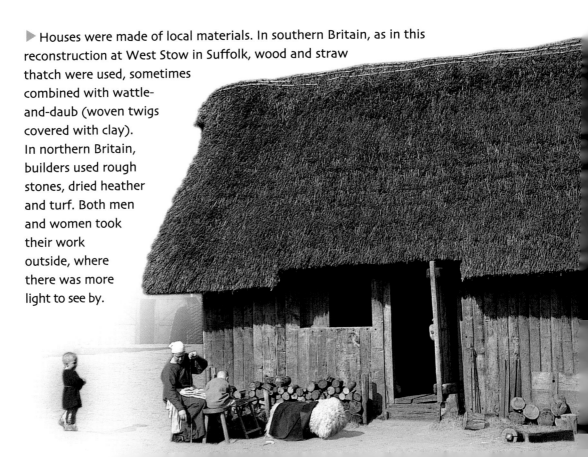

► Houses were made of local materials. In southern Britain, as in this reconstruction at West Stow in Suffolk, wood and straw thatch were used, sometimes combined with wattle-and-daub (woven twigs covered with clay). In northern Britain, builders used rough stones, dried heather and turf. Both men and women took their work outside, where there was more light to see by.

Workrooms and grand halls

In country areas, houses often had smaller buildings close by, used for storing food for the winter, or as workrooms for weaving, cheese-making, or mending farm tools. In towns, houses were much smaller and closer together. Chiefs liked to build grander houses, called halls, with at least one big room where they could feast with their warriors and honoured guests.

Inside a house

All houses were heated by open fires, which burned in **braziers**, or in hearths on the floor. There were no chimneys, so the smoke drifted up and slowly escaped through the thatch.

Furniture consisted of wooden tables, benches, and stools. Cooking pots were made of clay or iron and people ate off wooden bowls, picking up their food with their fingers. Beds were mattresses of feathers or straw, covered with woollen blankets or furs. In some Viking homes, beds were laid on platforms round the edge of the main room. There were no toilets. People used buckets or went outdoors.

No, not really. They were damp and had no windows to let in fresh air. In longhouses, manure from animals would have attracted disease-carrying flies. There were also fleas living in bedding, and on the dogs that liked to sleep by the fire. Houses were also full of smoke from fires. At night, sleepers ran the risk of being suffocated by a gas called carbon monoxide that is produced when fires burn up all the oxygen in a room.

▼ The remains of a large Viking farmhouse at Jarlshof, in Shetland. It was surrounded by cattle-byres, store rooms, workrooms, a corn-drying shed and a blacksmith's forge. The house was built using stones from an earlier Pictish building. (The Picts were Britons, living in Scotland, who fought against Viking invaders.)

Clothes

Saxon and Viking clothes were simple. For comfort, and to keep warm, people wore at least two layers – thin, lightweight *linen* or fine wool next to the skin, and thicker, heavier wool over the top.

Most clothes were woven by women and girls, using thread they had spun by hand, and were sewn using needles made of bone. They coloured the cloth with plant dyes made from moss, lichen, tree bark, gorse and heather. The colours produced were brown, pale red and rust, pale yellow and grey-blue.

Tunics and trousers

All men wore tunics which fell to just above their knees. Saxon trousers were usually close-fitting, but Viking men wore several different styles, such as loose and straight-legged, or baggy and pleated, or tucked into knee-length boots. For extra warmth and protection, all men wrapped strips of cloth over their trousers, from the ankles to the knees.

▼ In the reconstructed Saxon village of West Stow, a woman, dressed in Saxon style, is making flat, comfortable shoes out of leather. Her design is based on evidence surviving from over 1,000 years ago. The remains of several boots and shoes have been found by archaeologists at Saxon and Viking sites, where the cold, waterlogged soil has preserved them.

◀ A Saxon woman in York once wore these brightly coloured beads as a necklace. They were made by skilled craftworkers, who imported little squares of coloured glass from Italy, then melted them together to make their own designs.

Dresses and cloaks

Women's dresses were tied round the waist or chest with a belt of leather or embroidered cloth. Hems and necklines were decorated with woven braid or embroidery. Viking women also wore open-sided garments on top of their dresses, and held them in place with pairs of big, heavy brooches.

Cloaks were usually just lengths of woollen cloth draped round the shoulders, but rich people preferred cloaks sewn from strips of soft, warm fur.

Hairstyles

Saxon and Viking men cut their hair fairly short. Some had beards and drooping moustaches. In early Saxon times, women liked to wear gold, silver or embroidered head-bands and decorative veils. In later Saxon times, when most people had become Christian, married women covered their hair with a thick scarf or shawl. Many married Viking women also covered their hair.

JEWELLERY AND MAKE-UP

Saxons and Vikings all liked to wear jewellery. Chiefs gave their loyal soldiers silver arm-rings as rewards. Viking men also wore lucky charms. Both men and women liked to wear make-up produced from crushed earth and berries. Saxon men in Britain complained that Vikings were stealing their girlfriends, because the women found the Vikings were cleaner.

▼ Fine-toothed combs, made of carved, polished bone, from the Viking city of York. The Vikings used them to remove nits and lice from their hair.

Useful and Beautiful Crafts

Saxon and Viking families relied on expert craftworkers to make objects from metal, wood, bone, deer antler and stone. Most of these craftworkers lived in towns, but a few travelled round the country, offering their goods for sale.

Metalworkers were the most highly-respected craftspeople in Saxon and Viking times, and were often very rich. They made weapons, armour, knives and many different kinds of jewellery. Blacksmiths heated and hammered together thin strips of iron, then pulled and twisted them to create strong, very sharp blades. Jewellers wove fine gold and silver wire into delicate rings and bracelets, or cast heavier brooches out of bronze. They used precious stones and brightly-coloured **enamels** to decorate their work.

Brooch designs

Saxon designs were often **geometric**, or based on animal shapes. Viking patterns were more dramatic, with complicated, interlaced, swirling designs. Early Saxon men and women liked disc-shaped brooches; later Saxons chose brooches shaped like crosses or dragons.

◀ Wood was cheap and plentiful. It was used to make many different items, from boats to drinking bowls. In this reconstruction of a woodturner's workshop at the Jorvik Viking Centre in York, a craftsman is using a lathe and a sharp metal blade to shape the wood.

Brooches were the most popular Saxon jewellery. They were useful for fastening clothes – and they looked good! This splendid gold brooch, decorated with precious red garnet stones, was made for a wealthy Saxon in the sixth century. It is now in the British Museum.

Viking brooches were often oval. Many Viking women wore pairs of heavy, domed brooches. Britons preferred large, circular brooches, with very long, sharp pins.

Carving bones and stones

Other workers specialized in making combs, hairpins, spoons, dice and drinking horns from deer antlers and bone. Antler was very difficult to work, but could be cut and polished into very precise shapes. Bone was cheaper, but not as fine. Stonemasons carved tombstones and memorials. They also made everyday items such as bowls and lamps.

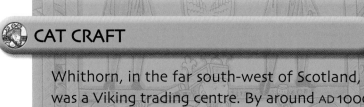

CAT CRAFT

Whithorn, in the far south-west of Scotland, was a Viking trading centre. By around AD 1000, many craftworkers lived there. They made leather goods, wooden board games, jewellery and antler and bone combs. They also bred large numbers of cats, which they killed and skinned for their fur.

▼ These chess pieces (now in the British Museum) were found on the Isle of Lewis, off Scotland. They were made from the long tusks of a walrus by Viking craftworkers. Each one has been carefully carved by hand, to show details of Viking people's clothes and appearance.

Towns and Trade

There were towns in Britain in Roman times. When Saxon settlers arrived, they took over many of these old towns. London and Southampton became busy ports, and Canterbury and York were religious centres. Winchester became the capital of King Alfred's kingdom of Wessex.

Foodstuffs grown on nearby farms were sold in town markets, and craftworkers had workshops there. Kings set up **mints** to make coins (often stamped with their portraits), and collected taxes from traders and their customers.

Foreign trade

Other goods came from much further away. The Saxons traded with glassmakers, metalworkers and swordsmiths from France and Germany. From Viking traders they bought luxury goods, such as furs and walrus tusks from Scandinavia, and silks and spices from the Middle East. The Vikings also sold slaves, captured from eastern Europe.

The growth of York

When Viking settlers arrived in Britain, they took over several towns. They made York the capital of their region, the Danelaw, building many new streets and houses and repairing the old Roman walls. In York, Viking settlers lived fairly peacefully alongside Saxon townspeople.

◄ Viking traders travelled vast distances across Europe, visiting local markets and important towns. Everywhere they went, they bought local goods to sell in distant lands. This Pictish brooch, made in northern Scotland, was found in Viking York.

◀ Silver coins from a Saxon hoard. Cutting coins into pieces created coins of a lesser value. When danger threatened – such as a Viking raid – Saxon people buried their treasures underground. Their hoard sometimes remained undiscovered for many hundreds of years.

▶ In this reconstruction from the Jorvik Viking Centre in York, traders and customers argue over payments at a busy street market. Although the Saxons and the Vikings made beautiful gold and silver coins, these were not widely used before around AD 1000. Before then, people bought goods using pieces of scrap silver, or bartered (swapped) them for items of equal value.

DEFENSIVE TOWNS

As part of his long struggle against the invading Vikings, Saxon King Alfred set up burghs (fortified towns) throughout his kingdom of Wessex. Each burgh was surrounded by a wall, of earth or stone, and had streets laid out in a neat grid pattern. Later, Viking settlers copied Alfred's example. They turned five towns in the Danelaw (Stamford, Lincoln, Nottingham, Leicester and Derby) into forts where they could seek refuge when Saxon armies attacked.

By the year AD 1000, over 10,000 people lived in York, making it the second largest city in Britain (after London). Merchants from many lands came to trade there, and it was also a great manufacturing centre. **Archaeologists** have found the remains of glass-blowing, metal-working and cloth-making industries, as well as workshops dealing in leather, bone, antlers and jet.

Entertainment and Punishment

Saxon and Viking people had to work very hard, but they also took time off to enjoy themselves. They liked many of the same entertainments – indoor games to exercise their minds, outdoor sports to build their strength, and storytelling, music and dancing.

Saxons and Vikings enjoyed playing indoor games – with dice, counters and boards – at all times of the year. In later Viking times, chess was popular.

Outdoor sports

In summer, children ran races, went swimming, and played games with bats and balls. Outdoor games for men included high-jump and archery, together with sports based on training for war such as spear-hurling, wrestling and stone-throwing. Everyone, including the women, watched horse-racing. They also enjoyed seeing sword-fights between champion warriors, and fights between angry stallions.

◀ The favourite Viking board-game was called 'hnefatafl' ('king's table'). It was rather like draughts. These pieces (found in York) were made from chalk and amber, although others were carved from walrus tusks, deer antlers and bones. The board shown here is a modern reconstruction.

▶ (Opposite) Entertainers like these, pictured by a Saxon artist in the 8th century, were employed by kings and great lords, or travelled from place to place, seeking food and shelter in return for performing. This manuscript is now in the British Library.

Evening entertainment

On dark winter evenings, families and friends huddled round cosy fires to listen to stories, tell jokes and riddles, or sing songs. Poets recited myths and legends full of dragons, giants and other scary monsters. Or they told tales of exciting adventures based on real events, such as battles and raids. Musicians played tunes on harps and pipes, and people sang or danced. In great halls, clowns, jugglers and acrobats amused the guests at feasts.

Trials and punishments

The Vikings were famously quarrelsome and seemed to like violence. So some of them probably enjoyed watching trials – and punishments. Saxon and Viking laws were severe. Liars had their tongues cut out, and people who made false coins had a hand chopped off. Most verdicts were decided by community opinion. Witnesses came forward, to swear to what they had seen. But for serious crimes, there might be a trial by ordeal. In some cases the accused person had to hold a piece of red-hot iron. If the burn festered, they were guilty. Other people might be thrown into cold water. If they sank they were innocent, but they probably drowned. If they floated, they were judged guilty.

Beliefs

When the Saxons first arrived in Britain, they honoured many different gods and goddesses. Each looked after a different part of life: Woden was the god of kings and poets, Hertha was the goddess of *fertility* and Tiw was the god of war.

The Saxons tried to enlist the help of each god by offering sacrifices. Usually, this meant killing living creatures. They also believed in magical beings like elves and dwarves, who could bring good fortune or cause disaster. They spoke to these through spells and charms.

▲ This 10th-century Viking carving on sandstone was found in County Durham. It shows Odin, the terrifying Viking god of wisdom, knowledge and war. Viking legends told how he rode a magic eight-legged horse, and was accompanied by two ravens named 'Thought' and 'Memory' who flew beside him, whispering into his ear.

Christianity hangs on

A few Roman-influenced Britons had been Christians. After the Romans left, small communities of Christians lived on, in the remote parts of Britain – Scotland, Ireland, northern England and Wales.

Saxons become Christian

In AD 597, Pope Gregory, leader of the Christian Church in Rome, sent a missionary to southern England. Saxon kings gradually became Christians. They built churches and monasteries, and encouraged many Christian scholars. Slowly, ordinary Saxon people became Christian, too.

READING AND WRITING

Most people in Saxon and Viking Britain could not read or write. There were a few experts who could understand an old north European alphabet known as **runes**, but this was mostly used for carving memorials or magic messages on wood and stone. Otherwise, rulers relied on poets to pass on information about great events and famous people in their songs.

However, Christian priests, monks and nuns kept alive the Roman tradition of reading and writing in Latin. Christian teachers became valued helpers to Saxon and Viking kings and queens. Some rulers demanded that Christian texts should be translated from Latin into languages spoken in Britain, so that everyone could understand them.

▲ This pottery burial urn, made in the 6th century, was found in Lincolnshire and is now in the British Museum. It was used to hold the ashes of a dead Saxon and is decorated with writing in runes. Being able to read and write was a very rare skill in Saxon and Viking times. People therefore believed that runes had magic powers.

Vikings attack Christian sites

The Viking religion was very similar to that of the early Saxons, and they worshipped many of the same gods. The Christian churches and monasteries in Britain were favourite targets for Viking raiders. But Saxons who defeated Viking warriors in battle usually demanded that they become Christians – if they wanted to stay alive!

▶ Christian monks and nuns, working in remote monasteries, copied Latin holy texts to create beautiful illuminated (illustrated) manuscripts, and also wrote new works of their own. This is the opening page of a history of Britain, written by Bede, a monk who lived in Northumberland around AD 730. Bede's history is one of our most important pieces of written evidence surviving from Saxon and Viking times. This copy is in the British Library.

War

The Saxons and Vikings had to fight to win land in Britain, and to keep it. Saxons fought against the Britons, and against Viking raiders. They also fought each other, as rival chiefs battled for the right to be king. When the Vikings arrived in Britain they had to fight against both Saxons and Britons.

Although they were often enemies, Saxon and Viking people shared many similar values, all based on war. They admired strength, daring and courage, and could be cruel to their enemies. They praised loyalty to chiefs and comrades in battle. They thought men should fight to defend their land, their families and their honour. They believed that fame, glory, riches and excitement were better than a long, dull, peaceful life.

Weapons and armour

Saxons and Vikings fought using similar weapons and armour. Their favourite weapons were spears and swords. Spear-tips and swords were made of iron. Spears had a long wooden shaft, and sword hilts and grips (handles) could be made of wood, bone, horn, leather or metals, and decorated with gold or silver. There were many different designs. Early Saxon swords were flat-bladed. Later swords had a groove down each side of the blade. To protect themselves, Saxon and Viking warriors carried wooden shields.

◀ History-lovers, dressed in Viking-style clothes and carrying copies of Viking weapons, pretend to fight a Viking battle. Re-enactments like this can help us find out a lot about the past – for example, how far a warrior could run carrying a heavy Viking shield, or how fast a Viking warship could sail.

This metal war-helmet (now in the British Museum) was found at the Sutton Hoo ship burial in Suffolk – one of the most important discoveries of Saxon objects ever made in Britain. It is decorated with a magic dragon – you can see its snout above the nose, and its wings over the eyes. It may have been worn by King Raedwald, who ruled the Saxon kingdom of East Anglia around AD 620.

Most shields were round, but late in Viking times some were kite-shaped. Kings and warlords could afford **chain-mail** tunics and helmets made of metal; ordinary soldiers wore thick, sleeveless cow-hide jackets and helmets made of boiled leather.

This gravestone from Lindisfarne Priory, carved around AD 800, shows Viking warriors brandishing their swords. Lindisfarne, an island off the northeast coast of England, was home to a community of Christian monks. It was one of the first places in Britain to be attacked by Viking raiders. They looted the church and terrified the monks.

Sickness, Death and Funerals

Compared with people in Europe today, the Saxons and Vikings did not live long. From the evidence of their skeletons it seems that many adults died before they were 35 and very few lived longer than 55 years. About half the children died before they were five years old.

Chief causes of death for men were accidents at sea or while farming, and injuries suffered when fighting. Childbirth was probably the main cause of death for younger women. Children mostly died from infections.

Healing the sick

Saxons and Vikings did not understand what caused disease, but they did their best to cure it, and to help injuries get better. Women were

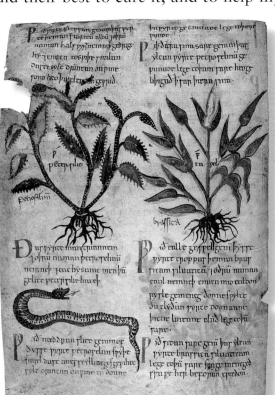

the chief healers. They braved battlefields to set broken bones and bandage wounds – using dried moss, which was naturally antiseptic. They also tried to protect their families by reciting magic spells and giving them lucky charms to wear.

◀ Saxon scribes (people who could write) collected as many herbal remedies as they could find, and wrote them down in books, adding helpful illustrations. This late Saxon manuscript is now in the British Library.

▼ Burial mounds (barrows) helped to keep safe the valuable grave-goods buried beside dead bodies for use in the next world. The barrows at Sutton Hoo preserved metal objects – like this gold and enamel shoulder clasp – as if they were newly-made. But the bones and flesh of King Raedwald, who was buried there, have been completely eaten away by the barrow's acid, sandy soil. This clasp is now in the British Museum.

Saxons and Vikings believed that most people would experience some sort of life after death. Viking myths and legends told how brave heroes who died in battle might be carried by warrior goddesses to Valhalla (the hall of the slain), to feast on pork and mead. Ordinary people were not so fortunate. They lived like shadows in an icy, misty world called Niflheim, ruled over by Hel, the goddess of the dead.

▼ After Viking people were converted to Christianity, they were buried in churches or nearby graveyards. Craftworkers carved stone monuments to mark their tombs. They still used Viking designs, like the wild beasts decorating this Viking Christian tomb at Brompton in Yorkshire.

Burial customs

Often the remedies failed and the patients died. Before the Saxons and Vikings were converted to Christianity, most bodies were buried with treasured possessions and many useful items for the dead to use in the next world. Important people were placed in ships, or in ship-shaped enclosures of stones, and their graves were marked by huge **barrows** or stone **cairns**.

Saxons living in northern and eastern England, and some early Vikings, preferred to cremate (burn) the bodies of their dead. The ashes were collected and buried in pottery urns. Once the Saxons and Vikings had become Christian, the bodies of the dead were usually buried close to churches and other Christian holy sites.

Saxon and Viking Survivals

The last Saxon and Viking kings ruled in Britain almost 1,000 years ago. Their power came to an end when Norman invaders – descended from Vikings who had settled in France – landed on the south coast of England in 1066. Their leader, nicknamed 'William the Conqueror', became King William I of England. He ruled the old Saxon kingdoms and the Danelaw as one united country, and gave Saxon and Viking land to his Norman lords.

In spite of this, many traces of Saxon and Viking Britain still survive today. We can see them in place names and in many common modern English words. We still enjoy Saxon adventure stories and tales of giants,

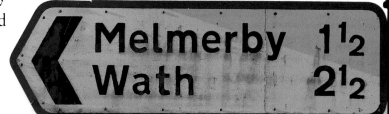

▲This modern roadsign from North Yorkshire shows two Viking place names that have survived until today. Place names that end in the letters *by* tell us that Vikings once farmed and kept cattle on the site.

monsters and magic from Viking myths and legends. We call several days of the week after Saxon and Viking gods: Tuesday (Tiw's day), Wednesday (Woden's day) and Thursday (Thor's day). People still have Saxon or Viking names. Edward, Hilda, Edith and Alfred were all popular among the Saxons. Viking favourites included Ingrid, Eric, Barney and Rolf.

Discovering what remains

In museums and heritage centres, we can also see many objects that the Saxons and Vikings left behind, such as silver coins, beautiful jewellery, fearsome weapons and carved stones.

◀ During the last 100 years, our knowledge of Saxon and Viking times has increased dramatically as archaeologists have carefully excavated many important sites. In this photo, you can see a Viking wall being uncovered in the Viking city of York.

▶ A few Viking customs have survived. The ceremonies of 'Up-Helly-Aa' are held in Shetland every January to mark the end of the Viking midwinter festival, called Yule. The local people set fire to a replica of a Viking ship.

Archaeologists have discovered many Saxon and Viking graves. There are Saxon charters (land documents), chronicles (history books) and religious manuscripts, and also a few Saxon churches. In remote parts of Britain, we can see the remains of Viking houses and farms.

Some people also like making accurate modern copies of Viking and Saxon clothes, dressing up in them, and acting out important events from Saxon and Viking history.

SAXON AND VIKING WORDS

When they settled in Britain, Saxons and Vikings brought their own languages with them. Over the years, these have combined with **Celtic**, Latin and Norman French words to create the English language we use today.

Words such as *field, fire, day, king* and *thumb* are all Saxon – so is the word *English*! *Egg, sky, skin, sister, happy* and *knife* are all Viking words.

Timeline

C.AD 200 First-known Saxon raids on Britain, then ruled by Rome.

C. 300 Romans recruit Saxon soldiers to fight against the Picts (from Scotland) and the Scots (from Ireland) who are attacking Roman Britain from the north.

407 End of Roman rule in Britain.

425-500 Saxon families migrate to Britain to settle.

C. 789 First-known Viking attack on England, at Portland, in the Saxon kingdom of Wessex.

795 First-known Viking attacks on Scotland and Ireland.

865 Vikings send Great Army from Denmark to invade England.

866 Vikings capture York, and make it their capital in England.

869-954 Viking families settle in northern and eastern England.

871-899 Reign of Saxon king Alfred the Great. He fights the Vikings and keeps them out of southern and western England.

1002 Saxons massacre many Vikings living in England.

1042 End of Viking rule in England.

1066 Normans from France invade England. End of Saxon rule.

1075 Vikings try to re-conquer England, but fail. Viking raids continue in Scotland.

1266 Vikings lose control of lands in Scotland, but keep islands of Orkney and Shetland.

1469 Orkney and Shetland become part of Scotland. End of Viking rule in Britain.

Places to Visit

Sutton Hoo, Woodbridge, Suffolk
Site of the most important Saxon burial so far discovered.

West Stow, Bury St Edmunds, Suffolk
Reconstructed Saxon village.

British Museum, London
Has many splendid Anglo-Saxon and Viking objects.

Jorvik Viking Centre, York
Reconstructed Viking town with many Viking objects on display.

Jarlshof, Sumburgh Head, Shetland
Well preserved remains of a Viking farming settlement. The Shetland Museum in Lerwick displays many of the finds from Jarlhof.

Tynwald, St Johns, Isle of Man
Site of the first-known Viking parliament in Britain.

Offa's Dyke
The largest Saxon defensive earthworks can still be seen in places along the border between England and Wales.

Glossary

archaeologist someone who digs up and studies ancient remains.

barrows huge mounds of earth heaped above graves.

brazier metal container filled with burning wood.

cairns cone-shaped mounds of stones used to mark graves and other important places.

Celtic of the Celts, the people who lived in Britain before the Romans.

chain-mail body armour made of joined metal rings.

enamel a glass-like, partly transparent coating used to decorate metal objects.

ferment go through a chemical process to produce alcohol from sugars and yeasts.

fertility the ability to produce more living things easily e.g. people producing children or trees producing fruit.

feud a long-lasting quarrel between families or tribes.

flax a plant from which linen fibres are made.

geometric using designs based on simple shapes such as circles and squares.

lathe a machine for shaping objects out of wood. It works by pressing a sharp metal blade against a spinning lump of wood. As the wood turns, the blade shaves thin layers off it.

linen a type of cloth, woven from the stalks of the flax plant, which grew in Britain.

mead a drink made from fermented honey and water.

mint the place where coins are made.

runes an ancient alphabet used in Saxon and Viking lands. It had 24 characters.

Books and Websites

Books

S Margeson, *Eyewitness Viking*, Dorling Kindersley, 2002

Peter Chrisp, *On the Trail of the Vikings in Britain*, Franklin Watts, 1999

B Williams, *The Saxons and Vikings*, Heinemann, 1995

Terry Deary, *The Smashing Saxons*, Scholastic, 2000

Philip Steele, *Step into the Viking World*, Lorenz, 1998

B Fowke, *What they don't tell you about the Anglo-Saxons*, Hodder Wayland, 1998

Websites

www.vikingjorvik.com
The site for recreated Viking York.

www.angelcynn.org.uk
Angelcynn (meaning 'the English People') is a Saxon re-enactment group.

www.vikings.ndirect.co.uk
A Viking re-enactment group.

www.regia.org
Regia Anglorum (meaning 'Kingdoms of the English') is a re-enactment group covering the years AD 950-1066.

www.bbc.co.uk/education/anglosaxons
A BBC site for 7-9 year olds.

www.bbc.co.uk/education/vikings
A BBC site for 7-9 year olds.

www.24hourmuseum.org.uk
Tells you about UK museums and galleries. Search by theme e.g. Vikings.

www.britarch.ac.uk/yac/
Young archaeologists' club (for 9-16s), with details of local clubs, events, competitions and more. Organised by the Council of British Archaeology.

Index